# If Your Days Looked Like Mine

Harleen Kaur

BookLeaf Publishing
India | USA | UK

Presentation by *BookLeaf Publishing*

Web: www.bookleafpub.com

E-mail: info@bookleafpub.com

ISBN: 9789357449007

First edition 2021

# DEDICATION

to my life's saviors - *a ma vie de coer entier.*

without a doubt, i would be dead today if it were not for you. instead i survive, because you have given me living parts of yourself.

at this moment, i can only keep bits of you alive in me, for i have lost myself. i hope that one day, i will learn to love life as you do.

# ACKNOWLEDGEMENT

an immense amount of gratitude to Rakaihya - a woman of few and chosen, but soulful words - for encouraging me to write at all. without your unending support, i would never have seriously contemplated writing poetry. thank you for listening to my first works, as i sat on a small yellow chair on my front porch, experimenting out loud with flow and grammar. thank you for believing that my words deserved to hold space in this big world. this collection would never have come to be if it weren't for you - i would not be who i am today if not for you.

another massive amount of gratitude to Daniya Mozaffar, for being my soul sister. thank you for constantly reassuring me that my writing was far more than "good enough." for showing me nothing but love and acceptance. for building a palace for me in your heart and allowing me to take up all that space. most importantly, for being there in every moment of torment, being a constant guiding light to pull through. for forever being there.

an immeasurable amount of gratitude to my late aunt Kamaljit Kaur, who i never knew. also a published Indian poetess post-mortem, she died far too young. perhaps, a piece of her lives in me. without my mother's stories of her, i would never have seen myself as a writer. i hope that one day when this life concludes, i get to meet her wherever she is and enjoy a cup of chai with her.

i owe an overflowing debt of thanks to my readers. if you picked up this book and thought it was worth your time, thank you. nothing gives me greater fulfillment knowing that you read my words and found them to resonate somewhere deep within you. without you, my works would never have seen daylight. i hope these poems make you feel heard rather than listened, echoed rather than suffocated. i hope you find peace. i hope you get to put it all down one day. i wish you nothing but an abundance of love.

# PREFACE

"Nothing ever ends poetically. It ends and we
turn it into poetry. All that blood was never once
beautiful. It was always just red."
- Kait Rokowski


i was 15 when i studied poetry for the first time.
i despised it.
i was 16 when i decided to write a book, if it was
the last thing i did before i died.
i was 22 when i picked up a journal and pencil.


i have etched into the following pages, a vivid
memory of what it feels like to survive 23 years
of life. as a consequence of having known a
lifetime of human suffering, there is blood,
brutality, and benevolence.


they say there's always sun after the rain,
something good to come out of even of life. so,
after having an intimate affair with depression
and death, i turned my burdens into poetry.


at the very least, i am one less mortal who fears
death.

# duality

To smell the salt in the ocean breeze.
To touch the petals of a sunflower.
When laughter sounds like wind chimes in the
spring.
To find home in your favorite eyes.
A canopy of sprawling emerald green trees.
To play peek-a-boo with the sun through the
leaves of spring.
To see a silhouette of the distant mountains in
the sun.
To know tomorrow is promised.
To smile so radiantly that it paints the sunrise.
To be pulled into an embrace after a deep
longing.
When joy leaves behind a residual tingling in
your toes and fingers.
To feel the Earth tilt ever so slightly on its axis
because you are loved.
To look at the stars in the sky and know they
reside in you too.
What beauty it is to be so human.

To feel the thundering crashes of the ocean
waves at shore.
To watch the grass go dry, brown, lifeless.
When agony stabs through your heart.
When you muffle your sobs with your pillow.
To embody rage and be unable to let it go.
To not be able to see past the clouds.
When the only escape is a hand through the
wall.
When loss stays an open wound that refuses to
heal.
To watch your dreams waltz past you from afar.
To be denied warmth, connection, love.
To keep carrying the burdens even as your knees
buckle.
When loneliness surrounds every last inch of
your living space.
To feel so much that you wish you did not have
the capacity to feel.
What a burden it is to be so human.

Lord,
I fear that
this beauty,
this burden,
this humanness -
it's too heavy to carry.
I fear that to live is a blessing,
and a curse.

# puzzle pieces

I find myself in parts,
like shards of a broken mirror,
scattered across the living room.
I see myself staring back at me,
something broken, jagged,
not wholly me.

I'm part hot, like the blazing sun -
sometimes I can mellow to a warm winter fire.
I'm part cold, like the freezing hail -
sometimes I can relax to an easy summer breeze.
I'm in balance, like the weather
for a walk during a beautiful spring day.

I'm part exhilaration,
like the perfect amalgamation of notes
in my favorite song -
I'm euphoria.
I'm part barren,
like the dry, tired earth that has cracked
under millions of trampling footsteps -
I'm hopeless.

I'm part vulnerable,
embracing my authenticity,

extending gentle grace to each wound.
I'm part guarded,
running away from the angry lash of a belt,
crawling back into my cage.

I'm half and half.
A bitter, cold-brew coffee: a twinge and a sting,
a wake-up call in the back of the throat.
A warm milk with sugar: comfort and relief.
a deep calling for me to return home.
Two halves that mix into a semi-whole,
but only find middle ground in a moderate
warm.
Bitter-sweet.

I'm the tiny puzzle pieces of a 1000-piece box
strewn across a large dining table.
I'm rough around the edges but beautiful in the
middle.
I'm unsure of what the whole picture is yet.
I wonder if I look good enough with the holes I
can't fill,
for I've lost some of myself to the world.

I'm part hurt:
Raging. Sobbing. Numb.
I'm part healed:
Peaceful. Laughing. Human.
Healed whispers and soothes,

but she's not enough,
because hurt howls louder.

I'm yearning for my parts and pieces
to connect. To link. To fit together
like something magnetic.
I keep wondering when
my footsteps will wander home.
Perhaps not until I feel whole -
but I'm not sure when that will be.
I'm afraid it will be never.

# dandelions

if i could be tiny enough
to marvel at the big world
standing tall over me.
i could use my hands to explore,
eyes wide and curious.

can i return to being young enough
for my grandpa to hold my hand
as cars clamor over one another?
to be pulled by a force larger than me,
my feet nearly floating in the air.

it would be a safe, happy world
if i could be ignorant
to the extents of evil,
to the depths of loss,
to the trauma of betrayal.

there was a time in my life in which
my hands were small enough
to hold clay and mold it into a vase.
if only my small hands could now
mold the earth into something to hold me.

if i could be naive enough
to think that i exist in two
because i see one of myself in the mirror.
for now, i know that i am only one -
and i wish she did not exist either.

to be in a field of dandelions
that tickle my stubby knees.
surrounded by tall grasses,
playing hide and seek with my hair.
the sun on my face - i would be okay.

# slowly

good things are slow to come.
*be patient. wait. it'll happen.*
but not all things
that come slowly
are good things.

we plant seeds, water them.
eventually they will become trees.
but i am not the tree -
i am the budding flower that was plucked,
thrown away, before i had the chance
to turn into a fruit.

rain does not thunder at once.
it collects in the clouds,
waiting for the opportunity to drizzle.
yet my years have hailed upon me,
raging and fierce, promising destruction -
i had to stand in it without an umbrella.

i have been running a slow marathon
to save up for a future life
that i don't even know exists yet.
for a tomorrow that is uncertain.
but if i were to perish tomorrow,

what then?

i have waited for good things
to come to me. i have been patient.
when will it be my turn at happiness?
perhaps never. because not all things
that come slowly
are good things.

# shame

I am dressed in shame.
It is the color of my cheeks
when a man calls after my long legs.
It is the color of my body,
when his hands grab at me,
dirtying my skin with his use.

It is the shade of rage
when my mother tells me
to have some shame
for not doing the housework,
for sitting with my legs uncrossed,
for acting unladylike.

It is the price I pay for pleasure in bed
when he whispers in my ear
with a glint of predator in his eyes,
"You are such a dirty, shameless woman."
It is also the price I pay for pain
when my mother shuns me away -
"Such a dirty, shameless woman
could not be my daughter."

It is the spear to my reputation,
when I am not tame,
submissive,
obedient.
I must not dare to have a mind of my own.
For being as I am
is a crime of nature.

It is the shade of my nail polish,
my lipstick, my eyeshadow,
that other men consider
an easy prey - a motel room,
cigar stubs, empty beer bottles,
sheets cinched at the hips -
"she's such a fun thing."

It is my existence
if I dare to love in the ways I desire.
A woman kissing a woman,
A man embracing a man.
A woman wanting to be a man,
A man choosing to be a woman.
Shame becomes my identity.

It is the burden of the secrets I carry,
family over everything -
all wrongdoings to the grave.
God forbid a stranger hears
of the crimes under this roof,

for shame would unfurl unto my blood,
haunting generations to come.

And should I choose to die,
to end my life violently,
or in silence,
to wear a shroud of white instead of shame -
it is the story of my life (my death),
"She was weak."
"She could've held on longer."
"What will we tell people if they ask why?"

They have dressed me in shame,
because I dared to have the audacity -
to speak,
to breathe,
to exist,
to be a woman -
to be.

# nightmares

tonight, tossing and turning
have their consequences.
while i struggle to fall asleep,
i think of all the things
you didn't do for me.

and i talk to God -
i ask Him where i went wrong,
what was my fault,
*what have i done to deserve this?*
i hear nothing back.

and when i finally drift off
into the middle ground that straddles
life and temporary death,
my mind lingers on the things
it is consumed by.

my suffering paints my dreams,
i feel the betrayal of your letdowns,
even in my nightmares.
i call out to you for help. and even
in my dreams, you won't listen to me.

i reach out my arms, begging for you

to turn around, to see me,
to hear me. to protect me.
to love me.
but i'm all alone.

you shake me awake. i realize,
you have not only consumed my life,
but you haunt my sleep, too.
and i think that i will never
again know peace.

and the only thoughts that ease me
back into some halfway slumber,
are that i was never destined
to make it this far. it's a miracle.
but look at the price i'm paying.

# small talk

I feel tired. I feel...
Devoid. Debilitated. Dead.
My heart feels too heavy to carry.
My chest feels like it's caving in on itself.
I fear that if I lean too far forward,
I might fall and never get back up,
that the earth might just swallow me whole,
and my footsteps will be forgotten,
like I never existed.
(Perhaps I was never meant to.)

If my shoulders are made of a ball and socket,
the socket is hollow; the ball has eroded
all of what was left to hold myself up.
Because I have yanked and tugged,
on every string that has ever bound me to this
world.
But the strings - they unraveled, snapped, broke.
The remaining pieces are strung across the sky,
the other ends now wrapping around my own
vocal cords.

I sigh, more often than I breathe.
I exhale little forget-me-nots into the air,
in hopes that someone is listening.

Perhaps my breath could become someone's air;
at least my existence would serve a purpose.
I walk through life as a vessel full of others,
but none of my own.
I come up empty at night, every night.

It is aggravating to be called brave, strong.
Where is the bravery in negotiating
with my own feet to stand on this ground,
to get myself off my knees as I beg for mercy?
Where is the strength in trying
to pull the sun out of the sky after it has set -
and failing - but they expected you to succeed,
regardless of the challenge?

I hold out my hands, palms facing upwards.
The lines on this roadmap of my fate
are too complex to read, too entangled,
and I cannot understand where my misery ends
and I begin.
I hold sand in my closed palms, squeezing the
grains together, but they escape
like fallen dreams that I cannot collect.
I wish to feel weak, for once.
To not have to hold myself.
I wish for someone else to hold me.
Just for a bit.

And even after writing my despair
into a dance of words,
to let these lines bleed the pain
out of my veins and onto this paper -
it does not do justice to the life I've lived.
I do not have a home. I do not have love.
*"How are you?"*
I do not feel tired.
But damn, do I wish I was just that.

# evanescence

Emptiness fills the chest,
My heart is hollow.
My forehead no longer crinkles
out of concern or worry.
Love no longer pours
out of this barren body.

The mind does not race
against time anymore,
to feed me fables of hate, rage, pain.
It chooses to wander,
to a different universe,
in search of home.

Laughs are akin to strangers -
knocking on doors of empty houses,
they are never to be found.
A smile flitters across the lips,
only to leave no trace, as does a rock
skipping across the surface of water.
If I sit too still, blink one too many times,
fatigue will swallow me whole.
Hope has left traces on my soul,
empty potholes too large to fill -

now voids of desolation.

The wish to disappear remains ever-present.
A desire awakens within me,
to be the slight scratch of a pencil,
or an ink blot that doesn't belong.
I could be erased, whited out -
no longer an annoyance or inconvenience.

The world feels full,
and I move through shapelessly, invisible.
My knees fold as the ground slips from under.
My hands search for a rope, a lifeline.
But I come up empty,
falling in slow motion.
God is nowhere to be found.

# september

fall has arrived at my doorstep,
bringing brown leaves and dreary skies.
it means that i am running out
of ways to shove my loneliness
back into the hole it keeps creeping out from.

the cloudy skies remind me
of the day that my dad's chest lay open
on the sidewalk of the park.
the faint scent of hesitant rain
in the air reminds me
of the heartbreak that leaks out
of every crevice of this house.

the cold ocean waters
no longer offer me any comfort
from the bright, blazing sun.
the seaweed around my ankles
feels like a forceful foothold
that i struggle to get out of -
i no longer wish to be anchored to this earth.

it means that there are few ways to find warmth
in the colors and space of nature -
and even fewer, in this even colder house.
it means that the floor's ceramic tiles
will dress me in cold,
thieving the remaining heat
from the soles of my feet.

it means that other families
will crowd around a table,
share a meal, dream of what will be -
while my face stares back at me
from the glass table,
nobody to share a meal with,
to reminisce of what was.
perhaps if i'm lucky, someone will notice I exist.

it means that every footstep feels heavier,
there is dust and death everywhere i walk -
loneliness is my only company,
and i return everywhere empty-handed.
nothing left to give.

it means that there is a black hole in my chest,
echoes of reverberating words and missteps.
it means that i must learn to trust the dark,
and hope that the lurkers do not yank me
into the chaos they so much enjoy wreaking.

it means that this city
has nothing left to give to me
nor i to it - nothing but bitter flashes
of who i was, who they were, what used to be.
it means i come up empty every night
when i lay wide awake,
tiny in this too-large bed,
fighting to find a purpose
to simply exist tomorrow.

it is the death of my bloom, my growth,
the beginning of my end.
i have nowhere to move, nowhere to go.
it is the home for my unbounded loneliness
to spill outwards and paint me
in abundant agony.
it is an avalanche
of my depleted, desolate, deserted.

i hope that i fall prey to this year's fall.
i wish to perish in the bitter winter to come;
i pray that i do not wake up next spring,
for i am simply unable
to survive another summer -
only for fall to arrive again.

# pov

Before I sleep, I pray.
For all the broken hearts in the world
that have been hurt - to be heard, to be healed.
I don't include myself -
I fear that I might count among the selfish.
*God, can you hear me?*
My heart - it's thrumming out its silent desires,
so words are not put to my misery.

I sleep, but I cannot be sure I dream.
Sometimes I thrash around
until I'm awake, but it's only daybreak.
A nanosecond of relief washes over me,
sleep takes me away again -
I don't have to face the world just yet.
I can hide for a few more hours.

I awaken around noon - I slept in too long.
I'm paralyzed by all the things I need to do.
*What time do I have to work today?*
*How long will it take for me to exercise?*
*Do I have to wash my hair today?*
The math in my head, it doesn't all add up.
I'd rather just... not.

I turn over to meet my pillow face-to-face.
It cradles me with softness and care
I know I won't find outside of my bed.
I breathe in the comfort,
I count down - *1... 2... 3.*
3 seconds of courage is all I need.
Yet, it's nowhere to be found.

I get up anyway, despite feeling incapacitated.
It's a war - my mind-to-muscle connection is
damaged.
I brush my teeth, change my clothes, exercise.
I feel somewhat accomplished.
But it feels as if the 10 hours of sleep
was all expended in 60 minutes.
*I have nothing left in me for the remainder of the
day.*
A warm shower is my only solace.

The white tile in my shower is cold to touch -
but it is the closest thing I feel to comfort.
I lean against the wall,
I breathe, *1... 2... 3...*
I can hear my blood pounding in my ears,
and my temples throb just as hard - a race
to which can make me feel more despair.
I sigh before I turn off the shower.
*I can't do this.*

I towel off, put my clothes on. Everything
around me moves in slow motion.
*I'm not ready for what's next.*
I brush my hair, moisturize my face.
I stare at my eyes a minute too long -
if eyes are windows to the soul,
my soul is long gone. It is fatigued - curled up
in the fetal position, somewhere far away from
me.

I settle in front of my computer.
I put on my best smile.
"Hi! How are you doing today?"
*I just have to get through the next hour.*
I'm hungry, I think. I force my feet
to walk 15 steps to the kitchen. They groan.
*I know, I'm tired too.*
I walk back. I put my game face back on.
The clock tells me I still have six more hours to
bedtime.

Work is done. I put away the computer.
I need to use the bathroom,
but my legs won't listen.
I plead with them,
bargain with them to just move.
I can't find it in me to move,
until my bladder screams.
I hold my head in my hands as I sit on the toilet.

I wonder when this will end. *Let's just stay here.*
Eventually, I get up - even though I'm not ready.

*Almost there.*
*Almost there.*
*Almost there.*
Dinner isn't very appealing.
My journal stares at me,
waiting for me to complain.
*I don't want to do this. I'm tired.* I write anyway.
I read a book to kill the remaining time.
Finally, bedtime.
Before I sleep, I pray.

# the days i never wanted

the ceiling hangs over me like the gallows tonight. you are ten feet away from me, but it feels like you are miles away. your chain around my neck has me in a chokehold tonight. do I choose you or do I go?

your love feels like an unhealed fracture, causing so much pain all the time. tell me, did your mother love you? do you know what a mother's love feels like? (maybe not, it is easier to not have than to have and miss). why can't you be mine? you prayed for me to grace your life for years, created me from blood, flesh, and womb, only to place conditions on my existence. how could you ask me to pay a price for every step I take forward without you? tell me, who hurt you so much that you cannot live without causing more pain? when did the world steal your peace? when did you start hating me so much? was it only when I was able to think for myself, or as early as when I could walk on my own two feet? how do you call this hatred of

yours a language of love? why is asking for your
love like walking over a bed of hot coals? if i
asked you to love me, would you laugh at me?
would you even think twice about why I would
say such a thing?

you are suffocating me. you have taken from me
more than you have given, and even that I ask,
why did you ever give in the first place if you
were going to take it all back? what is the price I
have to pay for you to stop hurting me? what
deal can we cut so that I can be happy? your
love is forcing me into corners that I don't fit
into and slamming me against walls that I don't
want to be squeezed against.

this one is dedicated to you. for all the days you
have given me. for the days i never wished for.
for the days you forced me to have.

stop loving me, woman. you are killing me.

# insanity personified

There are nights where I cycle through pain
to grief, to rage, and back to pain.
I'm struck by lightning.
Ropes unravel in me -
they pull me to either ends of the room,
toes to the window and fingers to the wall,
where they crawl and crawl,
looking for the right crevice to break through,
as I await the fall.

I tap on the glass,
"This isn't real," I soothe myself.
As my world comes crashing down,
and I hear the shards of my heart scatter
across the entirely too large floor of my chest,
it's too real to deny.
When my fingers tingle,
ready to yank out my hair, follicle by follicle,
and my own sobs strangle me,
it's too real to deny.

Pain echoes around in my head,
a boomerang bouncing off
the infinite barriers keeping guard.
but they don't hold too long,

When a tsunami tears them all down,
the boomerang turns into a blade
slicing through my chest.
My solid porcelain skin turns into a vent,
blood seeping.
Rage unfurls like pillows of smoke -
I'm blinded.
I'm submerged in the abyss of my own
desolation.
The night moves away in slow motion,
and the sun slithers onto the horizon.

# drinking honey

I went searching for love
in pages of books,
in leaves of trees,
in caresses of the tresses,
and then in you.

You lured me in,
promising me big todays,
and even brighter tomorrows.
I had not realized
I was looking for a savior.

Unknown to me was the
pain enlacing your promises,
misery tinging your music,
tragedy dripping from your tales,
venom hiding in your words.

You were my lifeline -
I desperately drank every last drop
of poison dripping from your lips.
Someday, I knew,
you would ruin me.

But I kept drinking anyway,
hoping one day,
I would be drinking honey.
That was when I knew
I had always loved my death more
than I would ever love you.

# confessions

this last hour of my life
is an outpouring of my helplessness.
as if my hands were molded
for annihilation, destruction, volatility.
i cannot be trusted in this moment.

i might crush it all to pieces,
shards jutting out of my palms.
and my hands hold me, my life,
my existence in a precarious balance.
soon, i will be fragmented across the floor.

my words have sliced my throat,
left my soul in tatters.
i exist in ribbons; there is dread
lacing around the shreds and threads.
i am nothing to me.

every thought drips abhorrent venom.
my mind is the hourglass,
a countdown to the ball drop.
i do not know what I want.
how much creativity does a rope hold?

my soul is disturbed. it is unhinged.
it seeks to pursue any avenue of peace.
light me up like fireworks,
a decadent display of colorful misery -
permit me to burst, explode, burn.

red has always been my favorite color.
which would be the better masterpiece:
painkillers in my palm, brains on the wall,
or blood in the tub?
which of my deaths makes the best decor?

the air in this room is suffocating me.
none of it pure; it is harder to breathe.
my lungs are too loud, too noisy,
and the clock on the wall ticks, ticks, ticks.
the pain - i see it - it will swallow me whole.

i am chasing death to the very end,
like an alcoholic and his favorite bottle.
life has squeezed the last of my essence
yet it demands of me more, more, and more.
i have nothing left to give.

*i am pleading for mercy, i beg you!*
i don't know who i'm yelling at to save me.
my words bounce off the walls,
distort into odd shapes, drift into the vacuum
of my own bottomless pit of despair.

there is nothing left in me to give.
i am hard-pressed to find peace.
and there is no telling
of what i may choose
in this moment.

# 70 x 7

Jesus saith unto him,
"I say not unto thee,
Until seven times: but,
Until seventy times seven."
(Matthew 18:21-22)

If I have borne the burden of responsibility
for a misgiving, a flaw, a sin, of your making.
If your finger pointed at me
as a compass does true north,
despite the rotten fruit in your own garden.
I forgive you.

If you tainted my name and reputation,
your venom as the forbidden fruit,
and I was turned away, shunned, denied.
If your words were spears to my ears,
or snakes that continue to slither across my soul.
I forgive you.

If you stole a virtue of mine,
without asking, telling, replacing.
For every wretched sob that has
pooled in my lead-filled lungs and escaped
my caged mouth - a prison of your making.

I forgive you.

If I took the bullet for you, bled for you,
but you couldn't even lend me
a shoulder, a hand, an ear.
If your wishes of evil against me were granted,
and the devil showed up on my doorstep.
I forgive you.

If you created a drought,
denied me water, told me my thirst was
a figment of my imagination.
If I humbly spread my hands out to you for help,
and you handed me a blade instead.
I forgive you.

If you tore into my chest, rib by rib,
parts of my heart shredded apart,
and swam leisurely in the pool of my blood.
If you doubted my heart made of gold,
because yours is blackened with soot.
I forgive you.

For every time you made me feel
that I did not belong in this place.
For every time you promised me home,
only to show me Hell again and again,
again and again and again.
I forgive you.

But I have sinned too,
by allowing you to wrong me.
So until I can forgive myself,
I forgive you
x 70.

# winter house

my mother tells me that 13
was my best. the golden age.
at 15, i fell in love.
with something terribly broken.
something that needed fixing.
i made one of day and night,
hoping to repair that wrecked heart,
maybe one day, love would pour out of it.

but it burned my hands,
scarred my lungs. it pushed
my head underwater, drowning me.
so i stopped fighting. i stopped fixing.
but my mother reached out a hand,
and i latched onto her arm if it saved me.
my mother tells me that 15
was my worst.

at 18, i found yet another thing
that my loving hands could hold.
it was not as fragile, volatile.
it was a small crack, hardly visible.
but once scratched, chips fell away.
and it was yet another object

i found myself trying to repair.

at 21, i left behind that broken project.
it was no longer my duty to fix it.
but my surroundings were in shambles.
if i had such a desire to fix the broken,
why not myself?
so i took my hands, pulled apart
my insides. built something better.
joined myself back with glitter glue.

yet, my mother tells me that 23,
is a repeat of my 15.
no new heights. no new horizons.
that i offer nothing to take pride in.
and suddenly, i collide into reason.
because i look at my mother -
and all my life, i have tried (and failed)
to fix the broken inside her.

if i were a mirror of my mother,
she would only see within me
what she can see of herself.
she chooses not to change -
therefore, she cannot see me.
i changed. 15, to 18,
to 21, to 23. as winter
to spring, to summer, to fall.

no two sunrises are the same,
nor are two sunsets.
and i wonder if change chooses us,
or if we choose change - and if the latter,
why does my mother not choose it?
i have chosen death before - i can again.
my mother could not be a mirror of me,
for no two forms of me would be the same.

but if i choose change,
then it is time to learn
to choose life over misery.
to choose life over survival.
to choose life over death.
it is time to learn,
how to survive - to live -
in this forever winter house of mine.

# money plant

once he crossed the oceans
my father kept a money plant
on the window sill of his apartment.
it grew into a small vine
and it was the only thing
he had to tend to.

when he married my mother,
promising her a lifetime,
she cared for the money plant
as if it were her own child.
over the years, it grew a luscious green,
died a deathly brown, and grew again.

when it was a beautiful vine,
my mother picked it off the window sill
and took the plant apart at the roots.
she tore it to pieces, promising it would regrow.
for a long while, my piece of the plant
stayed brown. it did not grow.

with enough sun, water, and time,
the leaves yellowed, the vine grew,
as surely and steadily as my heart beats.
and then it turned brown again,

as if it didn't think it could continue growing
when it was missing so much of itself.

but today, it sits on my window sill.
it is not growing - it is thriving.
the vine snakes around my curtains,
it's held up by strings
because beautiful things happen
when you support the growth of another's life.

when I see myself in the mirror,
I worry that I am only a piece
left of who I used to be.
after being held by supposedly loving arms,
those that snaked around my ribcage,
I have made a mess of myself on the carpet.

but if the money plant on my window sill
can live, survive. die. grow, thrive.
over 20 years of death and growth,
and between being torn to pieces,
I look at myself in the mirror and ask,
"why can't I?"

# for a lifetime

to have an innate understanding,
that you would kill for her.
that you would die for her.
to swear to love her.

but love is not meant
to mark the inevitable end,
nor the blissful beginning.
but to survive the grey in-between.

do not promise
to die for her, to kill for her;
perishing is easy. tell me,
would you dare to live for her?

# amor, love, pyaar

to love is just to love.
how divine is it
to only have one word
in every language, every tongue,
to describe our deepest desire.

a love as tender as a flower's first bloom
under the brilliant, warm, spring sun.
to sit in the same room, across one table.
it melts away the fear gripping your throat.
the afternoon glow washing over them.
their mere presence is a solace.

a love so powerful it has been threaded into you
stitch by stitch, into every last layer of you.
gravity anchors you not to the floor, but to them.
to know that among the many strings
that tie you to this life - their rope to you
is the thickest, the strongest. a pillar.

a love as passionate as disheveled hair,
bodies tangled up in the sheets.
a world that knows no end.
a way of being that transcends
the mortal cycles of life and death.

infinite. long-lasting. never-ending.

a love so sensitive to your existence -
it crawls into the dark holes with you,
sits next to you until you're ready to climb out.
it speaks languages of your breaths, sobs, sighs.
should they summon you by name,
you would arise gracefully even from your
grave.

a love so pure that every person
they have ever come across,
is blessed in their presence -
for they have seen and felt God.
neither water nor gold,
can compare to the vessel of heart.

a love so slow that it feels as if
there are miles more left to walk.
as the distance gets longer, the roads get windier.
but, the feeling gets sweeter,
as if it will never run out.
just as the sun and moon have taken turns -
never to stop, to continue till the end of time.

a love so fulfilling that your missing parts
no longer feel missing. something
that makes you want to live. to be thankful.
to feel peace in calamity,

to know silence in chaos.
a way that leaves no holes for intruders,
chases away all the worries. a home for the lost.

how marvelous is it to have one word -
to do it in so many ways,
to live in so many people,
and to know it ties us together today,
as it did yesterday, and will tomorrow.
a concept as timeless as the Creation.
to know that we are as much the universe,
as it is us.
to realize that perhaps
we are all each other, just in different ways.
to understand that as we seek each other,
maybe we have just been seeking
ourselves.

# une dévouement

3 am - it's raining outside,
and tonight, i'm thinking of you.
i am to be absorbed
in the love of the Lord,
and perhaps that is why
it has been so easy to love you.

you're the anchor to my soul,
holding me so I don't drift.
in a brutal, cold world
that is used to letting go,
you stay. you listen. you comfort.
you love.

to put my love for you into words
would compare to the fragrance
of the freshly wet earth.
an end to a longing,
a way of feeling complete.
the end of missing someone.

and i am luckier than anyone else,
to have you in my life.
I am safe with you
the way that stars are among the clouds.

and even if the dark skies hover too low,
your light will break through to guide me.

the rain has come to an end tonight;
it is only the sound of pipes leaking
into the ground that is testimony.
but the earth remains wet,
imbued in the devotion of the skies -
the same way I will continue to love you.

know that tonight, as i fall asleep
I count my blessings to Him -
and your name unabashedly
will arise to my lips,
for you are His greatest gift to me
in eternity, til death do us part.

# the chosen one

on my thirteenth birthday,
my father gifted me a pair
of silver anklets that jingle
like Christmas bells.
and I have not taken them off since.
their jingle marks my arrival in a room.
but they do not know that with each step,
I carry my father with me.

after my incessant fussing
over many cheap, rusty necklaces,
my mother unclasped her chain
and dressed me in gold.
some days, it feels like a noose
that may strangle me.
but most days, it sits above my heart
and reminds me of where I come from.

my sister and I wear a set of twin rings.
and even when the distances between us
feel infinite, I cannot bring myself
to remove her from my left hand -
I feel incomplete.
my brother will never say "I love you"
but he will wake at dawn

to buy me a pair of sneakers that I'd love -
and teach me how to walk without creasing
them.

my sisters from different mothers and blood;
one gave me a ring - two intertwined ropes,
promising me her presence in spirit
everywhere I go -
she has traveled on my right hand since 23.
the other bought me my favorite sweater
to wear when I feel the chill in my bones,
because I told her I could not afford to buy it.
worn last winter, it'll be worn again every year.

to be adorned in the love of others
is to be full of the Creator's love.
I am incomplete without
the people who I love, who love me.
I am a composition of others' love -
how fortunate am I to live a life
where people have chosen me
again,
again,
again,
and again.